Or.
Writing

(and other mysteries)

Steve Page

Cover Photo by Patrick Fore @ unsplash.com

First Printing: 2023

ISBN: 9798390373514

Imprint: Independently Published

What?

Steve's a writer. Sometimes he writes poems about the writing experience. This collection brings together poems on the writing process and on the thinking that precedes it.

Who?

Steve lives in Ealing and worships at Redeemer London each Sunday at the University of West London. He 'worships with a pen in his hand' and takes inspiration for his poetry wherever it rears its head.

Why?

To hopefully lift the veil on the writing experience – its joys and its challenges.

Why now?

In 2019 Steve included 'Life of a writer' poems within the collection 'Not Too Old To Dance'. These are those, along with the poems that follow the same theme.

Introduction / Credits

I started taking writing seriously in poetry classes run by The Poetry School in the early noughties. I learned a lot very quickly through the generosity of the tutors and fellow writers on those courses. Since then, I've had the pleasure of making connections with other writers local to me and across the UK, taking inspiration from conversations and email exchanges. A special thanks to Jonny Baker at Proost Publishing for including my poetry in their collection, 'Learning To Love' and giving me confidence in my writing. And thank you to the writing charity, Arvon, whose retreats have been a Godsend. I've also greatly benefited from the encouragement of the tribe of writers at hellopoetry.com – a worldwide gathering of poets who never fail to amaze me with their passions and talent.

More recently I've had the pleasure of rubbing shoulders with the creative folk within my local church (see RedeemerLondon.org), who have consistently showered me with their love and support over the past 9+ years.

I guess what I'm saying is that the writing process for me has not just been a solitary one. It's also been a journey in the company of likeminded and likehearted individuals who continue to stimulate me and the words that flow from my keyboard and pen.

This is for them.

"If you want to change the world, pick up your pen and write...."
Martin Luther.

(and put it where it can be read)
Steve Page.

Poetic Licence

We've got a licence to be poetic
and we're not afraid to use it
Can we stop you for a moment
cos we think you need to hear this

We can work with a little discord
We can dance with juxtaposition
We're even sometimes partial
to suggestion by omission.

We've got a licence to be poetic
and we're not afraid to use it
We've got a mouthful of metaphor
and little time to chew it

We get giggly with similes
and silly with alliteration
We're warning you now
We're devoted to proper diction.

We've got a licence to be poetic
and we're not afraid to use it
so, give us some extra space
cos we think I'm going to lose it

We're in love with eloquence
and we fawn for fluency
We can't get near enough
of off-beat rhythmic lunacy.

We've got a licence to be poetic
and we're not afraid to use it
but we use it for the good
and avoid the usual nasty

We're tired of hearing hate
bred from petty bitterness
We're looking to collaborate
with poets with forgiveness.

We've got a licence to be poetic
and we're not afraid to use it
so, let's sit down and talk
cos we think you need to hear this.

Re-written for a spoken word event organised by Redeemer London.

Art work

The ground work, the art work,

the craft work, the hard work,

the life work of a working poet

works on long after the pen rests

and the mind drifts

to pouring wine and making dinner

at the close of the journal

at the close of another working day

The words dance on, the mind works on –

fermenting, gestating, word-playing

while the pen and the journal lie waiting

ready for the release of fresh ink

at the start of another working day

It's impossible to switch a writer's brain off

– ideas don't respect boundaries.

Stand Up Poetry

Step up to the mic and strike first with a smile of one-liners,
with observations or tales that surprise and beguile us.
For a smile will disable us
while your lines slide in behind us,
almost whispering, selecting the sharp-soft phrases
that will best penetrate our well-guarded places.

Look with innocence into our faces,
turn our minds stage by stages,
persuade with insights, with stories of real life,
peppered with shared joys and familiar life strife.

Then when you follow through and strike with a punchline,
we'll have no defence left and have no time to decline
the good sense found in your good food for thought,
our breath that's caught, with a sudden realised stop,
looking again at our lives,
with furtive smiles of dawning delight
at this shed light on shared lives
found in your softly spoken (amplified) lines.

Do it right when you step up to the mic
and we just might let you change our minds.

The unfinished poem

I'm not finished yet, I'm nowhere near complete
you know I'm not near done, you know I'm not replete

so, now's the perfect time to pause and let me go
time to pack away, take that towel and throw -

put me in a drawer, stand up and walk away
go on and fill the kettle, or try that new café

come back some time later, then look at me afresh
maybe ask your closest friend to suggest some more or less

once you've returned you won't be surprised to find
you're still not satisfied and can't get peace of mind

I'm art, I'm not a race; there is no finish line
so please don't overwork me,

I'm unfinished by design

'Art is never finished, only abandoned.'

– quote attributed to Leonardo da Vinci.

I think in 3D

I think in 3D,
I need real depth you see

I need more than one surface
to do my thoughts justice

I need three perspectives
to avoid a disservice
to any ideas that swim their way
up to my disturbed surface.

I'm not saying my thoughts are wordless
just that the words are surplus
to the primary purpose of the thoughts
that win that struggle
and that finally find a thoughtful purchase
to become rooted and to bear fruit
to fulfil their true purpose.

I think in 3D IMAX
– and its scares me.

Do you think in words or images?

Hidden rages

I'll be entirely honest, but not completely true
I'll be true to my heart, but not always true to you

some of my words will reflect much of what I feel
while some other lines are more contrived to conceal

you see a poet uses words to bear their deepest feelings,
look again and you'll see something deeper redder bleeding

read again between the lines of the fresher tender cuts
you'll brush a slower finger over old wounds long untouched

you may detect my untold stories seeping through the pages
you may find a heart like yours where an older passion rages

Hidden rages don't easily find words.

Things unsaid

Some things I will not say
I will not form those words
Lest they be heard
Lest they be believed
and the truth of self
be known.

No, some things I will not say
I'll keep their silence
Keep my distance
and stay quiet
safe on this side
of my deceit.

Poems that dance

The best poems avoid eye contact.

Just before you find their rhythm,
catch their direction,
they dance away,
and you watch their beauty, leaving

you full of wanting, wishing
you knew the steps, hoping
you might keep up, wondering
where they led, leaving
you to tap your feet, missing
every third or fourth beat, kidding
yourself that you too
could be sliding, shuffling
and maybe grasping the sway,

but they dance away, and you stay,
while your eyes follow.

Caroline Bird (in interview):

"Some poems won't keep eye contact."

Denial

At your denial
you were at your creative all-time-best
as you added vivid detail
that distracted and buried
the facts beneath a story that captured
our imagination rather than releasing
the truth of the situation and risking
the shame of the truer declaration lying
a few lines beneath your masterly woven
(but ultimately deceptive)
late night conversation.

And you left us none the wiser.

Caroline Bird @ Arvon:

"Denial is so imaginative"

Collaborator

He snarled at me, accusation embedded into each word –

"I thought I knew you, I thought I could trust you, but you're
nothing like I thought. How can you bear to live with
yourself! How can you not feel sick! - Collaborator!"

He expelled that last word as if he would be the one to vomit.

"You gave in. While the rest of us struggled on, you gave in.
We thought you were with us, but all along you had betrayed
us. You betrayed yourself!

"You didn't write that alone! "You had a partner – didn't you!

"DIDN'T YOU!"

I paused not sure how to respond. It was true, I couldn't deny
it. I had stopped working alone. I had - *collaborated*.

I had fallen in step with another writer –

and it had felt great!

Collaborator isn't always a dirty word.

Story

Sometimes reality is just too much, and I pop out for a while. I step into a story and I make it my own. A space shaped just for me.

Then I gently expand my space to accommodate my latest imaginings. I push and stretch, build and take new ground with every new thought, with every fresh fruit of each branch of each path.

And once I've created sufficient space, I invite my friends, my close friends, my network family to join me and to join my story and so to enjoy these strange fruits of my imaginings.

And we feast.

I need to write. It's where I get to call the shots.

Singing from the heart

I've been singing high up in my head
not aware I have a choice
not knowing in my heart of hearts
I've got a bigger voice –

that breath by breath, beat by beat
I'm able to release
in time with my heart's moving
the next movement of my suite

Recipe for creativity

"A grain of madness is the best of art."

Second best
is a handful of heartbreak
on a baked base of isolation
with a drizzle of self-reflection.

First line is a quote from a movie: At Eternity's Gate.

Treacle

Time here is treacle –

it's thick and syrupy,
a rich golden glow that envelopes the spoon
while flowing over the edges inevitably leaving a trail
a thread if you will,
that will never be chased down or scooped up
without leaving a sticky sweet trace that will last days
before it fully fades to a savoured memory.

Time here is golden treacle.

Reflections on a poets' retreat. Golden.

Speed of thought

I sit thinking a little faster than the speed of my penning,
thereby having to repeatedly press pause on my thoughts to
let the ball of blue catch up with the image / the sound of the
phrase in my mind / on my quiet tongue that flows fast down
my right arm into my slow fingers and out into the ball point
that hits the page with part-satisfied impatience

And in that pause, resisting the urge to edit / to revise / to
reform the original thought that is crying out to become
embedded in the page / begging to be seen / to be loved and so
to sit and to stare back at its origin, safe in the curated space to
stay / to settle and perhaps to become part of something bigger
/ longer / older, something of possibly permanent beauty.

And having gotten over that feint-ruled line, my first thoughts
face the risk of being transposed / transformed by typing
thumbs before becoming something that will last on a plain
white screen and later be posted at the speed of competing
broad bands into a worldwide cloud of words.

Later, having hovered / waited, my wet words just might find
a place to soak / to stain / to marinate and later be memorised
perchance recited at a more appropriate speed within a crowd
of like-minded minds and perhaps for a phrase to lodge / to be
recalled by another / to form part of something that fate
redirects through a ball of blue, back into the universal flow.

On my cycle of thoughts and articulated phrases.

Big Art

Big art
bouncing, cushioning,
resonating, in-phasing.

Small piece-by-piece-making,

patch-working, ingredient-ing,
folding, combining, conjoining,
absorbing,

- collaborating.

Becoming Big Art.

Riffing off a phrase heard on the radio:

'Big art is the act of collaboration.'

The Jazz

And where do you keep the jazz?

Where do you store the melancholy,
the self-reflection
and the escape.

Direct me to the place you keep
your inner, your deeper,
your best kept back

and let's sit and explore,
let's jazz and coalesce
into a more honest
and more innovative
improv.

Sparked by a scene from a novel 'Moon over Soho'
by Ben Aaronovitch.

Finding My Voice

"Once you have found it
keep your Voice on you at all times,"
my Uncle told me,
"you never know when you might need it.
Do not entrust it to anyone else -
they won't value it the way that you do.

"And do not leave your Voice
where they can steal it,
but slip it in your inside breast pocket,
close to your quiet heart -
where you can reach for it
at a moment's notice,

and when the moment comes,
be sure to take it out with a steady hand
and you let them see
that your Voice is not lost,
it is not tired,
that it lies ready

you show them that it is willing
to speak truth to power,
to voice comfort to the powerless
and sing in chorus with quieter voices."

And he patted my hand,
"You'll know. You'll know."

Years later,
when I found my Voice
far from where my Uncle had sat,
I knew it was mine
from its familiar shape and weight in my throat,
from the way it resonated
with the call I had suppressed
and the way it chimed
with the voices of those who chose
to stand with me.

And now that I've found it,
I exercise my Voice in song,
I practice it in comfort
and I school it in truth

and I always keep it close
to our quiet hearts
where they cannot steal it from us.

'Finding my voice' takes time.
I recommend 'Search for My Voice' by Felicity Ann Alma and
'A Portable Paradise' by Roger Robinson.

Ends

Not reaching
Not arriving at

but *going through,*
continuing past
this end

on to the next

ready for any number of ends that I may meet and greet and
then pass, thanking them, but not being held by them.

Maye saddened by them,
but not brought down by them,

rather, finding myself a lot stronger and a little wiser,
I walk on to find my end that will always be
ahead of me, past these ends.

"I think it's this hope that keeps me going through difficult ends."
Amy Page.
https://tinyletter.com/amypage/archive

Not totally lost in translation

Being compromised
between the original and the possible

losing the beat
and a little of the rhythm,
even the form,

as the pulled words
fall afresh,
fall short of English,
far from the tree,

but cousin enough
to retain a likeness,

and still echo a piece of me.

Listening to poets talk about the challenges of translating poetry.

Unreliable

I write for the unreliable reader,
the one who reads what they want,
whether they want
and how they want
- not reliably reading though my eyes
not carefully abiding with
my well-placed breaks in line,
my enjambments,
the separation of themes into stanzas
or even a subtle semicolon.

I write for you
and entrust all this to you.
So just turn the page.

To the reader

You complete me and do so
in every sound you now mouth,
with every movement of your tongue,
every muscle's adjustment
to effect fresh shape to these phrases,
in every quick, shallow breath
giving sudden pause and turn
to the next silence.

You complete me at this reading
and so I am deaf to the closing,
blind to the ending you gift me
and ignorant of the next stair,
with no balustrade to steady,
where you leave this older me
to rise to find, first-hand,
the landing that completes me.

triggered by Walt Whitman's 'To You'.
"...now I place my hand upon you, that you be my poem..."

Story Told

Not pen to paper nor digit to key,
but eye to eye and hand to hand,
with a firm grip on our reality.

With half-empty mouths and full-empty ears,
we understand that it has to be us
voicing our two converging histories.

Exploring what it is to be you,
what it is to be me
and what we two can be together
in the next chapter of our come-together,
unfiltered, unashamed,
and unheard stories.

Story telling pre-dates the written word.

Story tellers are who we have always been.

A muddy thing

Is truth now a muddy thing?
Is that how we prefer it to be?
Is truth a muddy clay
ready to be shaped 'til it pleases me?

Is truth now a muddy thing
thick and deep, hiding what's beneath?
Designed to hide my face
as I seek a private deceit?

Is truth now a muddy thing,
wet, heavy with grit and cold?
Can I scrap it off my boot,
safe outside my safe threshold?

Is truth now a muddy thing,
slowing me wading ashore?
Immune to curses and stumbles,
dragging me to the floor?

If truth is now a muddy thing
can I filter it and sieve?
Can I find a rock that's not been eroded?
Will I still find true truth within?

I spent my day

I spent my day breathing life
into my memories.

I often walk or sit among them.
I give them the attention they ask for
to maintain their roots.

I administer the moisture they desire
to retain their colour,
their scent.

I know they aren't what they used to be,
but they grow with me
and give me hope for more,
more beauty
more life
and more to live for.

I spent my day with my memories.

God is a poet

This is my anthology of choice.
This is where I hear God's voice -
wrapped in eloquent grace,
punctuated with tearful praise.

User manual and admonishment.
Hope and encouragement.
Stories of enemies and friends
where all battles end
in the end.

This is my anthology of choice.
This is where I hear God's voice.
Soft like the call of a lover.
Earnest like the tears of an open-armed Father.
Substituting justice for forgiveness.
Love Joy Peace and Patience.

This is my anthology,
my compendium of choice.

This is where I hear God's stanza'd voice.
Where his words collide with my joy.
Where words can fly.

Tonight, God is a poet.

A response to Robert Alter's 'The Art of Biblical Poetry'
and riffing off the song, 'God is a DJ' (Faithless)

Content

If I was content
I wouldn't write
Create
Sing
Love

or even look behind the veil.

If I was content
I would just be silent and still.

Lord, save me
from content.

Few of my friends

Few of my best friends
are poets

They live different
They walk faster
They're more organised
They have more friends

They are readers (occasionally)
And writers (spasmodically)
- never pathologically

My best friends
are breakers of silence

and I need them more
than they need me

I lift my pen

I lift my pen at the scent of the coming rain.
The wind rises, and I sense the pain gathering strength
and after a beat or two, the drizzle scouts my face
- but I smile.

I have my compass, the North Star
and the maps I made before.
I can still climb this new stanza
navigate past the memorials,
through to the meadows beyond
and I can rest there, refill my pen with the rain
and write again.

Memory and New

Place the pen on the page before inspiration hits – that's important. You write – that's what you do.

And as the pen moves, a combination of Memory and New combine, they interact with the catalyst called inspiration and you'll find that the further the process is allowed to progress, the more the New takes hold and Memory drops to a whisper and before your mind can comprehend the words, you find an unexpected theme. This time it's about the evil of Memory and how it needs to be subdued / reduced, put in its rightful place so that the New can breathe / can grow / create a new Memory that will one day abdicate space to the next generation of New.

One day we might find there's no heir, no one who cares enough to continue the line, but until that day we'll have generation after generation of New - each slowly growing old, gradually fading thin and becoming a memory that knows its space and gives way.

I pause. That's always a mistake. To Pause. That's when Memory sneaks back in, raising itself above its whisper, giving pause to the New and raising an appetite for a brew which lifts the pen...

And a memory of grandma's blueberry jam on madeira cake takes me to the kitchen.

Bending, not broken

The arc is long and it bends towards -
and then away and seems to circumvent the gateway to better,
to truer and rather it dips and, for some unfathomable reason,
detours through bone aching drivel which we sit through lest
we cause offence and in defence we smile until someone offers
a glass and we can distract the conversation to something real
and relevant and alive – preferably with alcohol.

The arc is long and it bends towards -
and then it rainbows, so you'd think that there'd be no excuse
but to look up and wonder at the way in which each colour
blends, leaving no distinct edge, no start or finish, leaving you
in no doubt why spectrum is an apt term to capture diversity
with harmony, and leaving you staring curiously while the
world walks on, heads down, focusing on the familiarity of
their grey, woollen comfort zones.

The arc is long and it bends towards -
the other side, it crosses divides, where bridges were long
fractured, and diversions had left the land desolate - and now
we can repopulate, reconnect and proliferate something that
binds a kindlier fraternity wedded to justice indiscriminately.

The arc is long,
bending, not broken.

Martin Luther King Jnr:
"the arc of the moral universe is long, but it bends toward justice."

Burdened

The paper weight will hold
my ink down
in a way my fluidity never could.

No matter how violent
my metaphor, how heady
my imagery, how blistering
my narrative - it will hold
the reader's attention,
ensuring my thoughts reach
each reader's own resolution
a little before the weight shifts
and the burden of their eyes falls
heavy on the turn
of the page

and then their eyes will lift,
burdened with new meaning.

Censure

A life of self-censure is life
on a knife's edge,
balancing, filtering,
hesitating, holding self back,
placing pitiful tack over ruthless honesty,
hedging truth, seeking to closet self
and not out of self-modesty,
but more honestly, out of self-doubt,
coupled with arguably
some reluctant scam artistry.

A life of fearful self-censure
is no life at all -
I think you'd agree.

Short

To make a long story short

is to make a poem.

Handrail

Poetry can hand me
a handrail for the steps down,
can steady me for the unexplored depths.

Poetry can hand me confidence
that I am not alone
that there are words
gifting markers of hope
leading me back to the surface
should I choose it.

Mental health has its ups and downs.

Handrails help.

Every Moment Inspired

A rabbit with a pipe
sits like they own their space
like there's nothing that might move them
unless they acquiesce,
like they have no better things to do
than do exactly what they're doing
and they're doing what they do best

- contemplating the next word, the next note,
the next sweep of their pen,
the next throw of the clay
and the colour they have chosen to inject
into the next page, the next dye,
the next stitch, beat, thread, chapter, adventure
that their maker has placed in their mind's eye
and it's then that I realise
that in every moment they're carefully holding
a myriad of holy inspirations
and contemplating their ordering so that beauty may abound
so that their beautiful God may breath out
yet more of the Creation.

(The rabbit is a reference to the Rabbit Room – see
https://www.hutchmootuk.com/hutchmoot-uk-2023)

Note to self

If you want to learn to play the guitar, you find a tutorial book, you learn the chords, the rhythms, the techniques and you practice, practice, practice. Sometimes its hard work. More often it's fun.

If you want to write songs, you write. Some are just play, with no real meaning; some songs express your heart. Both are worthwhile.

Some sound good and connect with others. Some don't.

That's fine.

If you stop playing, if you stop writing you will get rusty. But you can pick it up again.

Poetry is the same.

Keep writing.

A poem is a flawed thing

A poem is a flawed thing
made by damaged hands,
from thoughts yet complete,
in words unsound,

but close, like a whisper away,
(as close as a line-break)
to the heart of something.

The Unknown

Treasure the unknown, the unseen
for there you find
untold story,
unsung song
and unimagined vistas
waiting to greet us.

And, yes, some of the paths are long,
the climbs hard,
the adventures testing,
but we have good counsel,
and good company

and they will take us through
the deep story to the high chorus
where the harmony will be sweet.

Also from Steve Page

If you enjoyed this collection, you just might enjoy

Not Too Big To Weep;

Not Too Old To Dance;

Not Too Soon For Christmas;

Father is a Verb;

Fruity Poetry;

Wisdom Poetry;

Real Christmas Poetry;

Hollow Egg. Empty Grave; and

Poetry @ Prayer.

If you still want more, you can find me amongst a world-wide crowd of poets on hellopoetry.com

And if you're into prose try:

Deborah's Daughter; and

A man walks into a bar.

Printed in Great Britain
by Amazon

21546801R00031